SKY DIVING

John Allan

www.hungrytomato.com

First published in 2022 by Hungry Tomato Ltd.

F1, Old Bakery Studios, Blewetts Wharf, Malpas Road,
Truro, Cornwall, TR1 1QH, UK

A CIP catalogue record for this book is available from the British Library.

Manufactured in the USA.

ISBN 978 1 914087 21 9

Picture credits
(t=top; b=bottom; c=center; l=left; r=right)

Erik Aasbarg: 33b. Airbourne Systems: 11t. Airtec: 17t. Alti-2: 17c. Chris Barry/Action Plus: 18t. Felix Baumgartner: 40. Hans Berggren: 17b, 29b. Bettmann/Corbis: 9cl. Darren Birkin: 27b. Willy Boeykens: 5b, 14t, 25t, 26/27t, 28.. Bone Head: 14b. J C Colclasure: 21t. Corbis: 8t. Tony Danbury: 35t. Jay Epstein: 41b. F.A.I.: 60b. Andy Ford: 19c, 38t. Oliver Furrer: 39tr. Sarah Hall: 30b, 31br. Mark Harris: 24t, 43t. Tony Hathaway: 2. Ian (Milko) Hodgkinson: 45t. Ash Hollick: 35b. Simon Hughes: 34. iStock: OFC background. Jump Shop: 15t. Jupiter Images/Thomas Ulrich: 41t. Norman Kent: 4b, 23br, 42. Keith MacBeth: 22/23t. Peter Male: 36. Anton Malevsky: 22b. Neil McLaren: 11b. Mike Mumford: 9tr. Francisco Neri: 12/13t, 20t, 21cl. Craig O'Brian: 29t, 38t. Dean O'Flaherty: 4/5t, 32/33t. Johnny Panakis: 44. Patrick Passe: 39cl. Photolibrary: 1, 25c. Shutterstock: OFC (skydiver), 3, 16, 46. Sky High Entertainment Movies: 45b. Barbara Sokol/Beck Isle Museum/Sydney Smith: 7b. Square One: 15cr. James Stevenson: 30/31t. Jack Sullivan/ Alamy: 13b. ticktock Media Archive: 19t. Total Control: 15bl. Gary Wainwright: 12b. 26b, 32b. Simon Ward, sward@airkix.com: 37b, 43b. Wikipedia: 6, 7t.

Every effort has been made to trace copyright holders, and we apologize in advance for any omissions. We would be pleased to insert the appropriate acknowledgements in any subsequent edition of this publication.

CONTENTS

INTRODUCTION

OVERVIEW

Skydiving means diving into the sky from an aircraft, helicopter or balloon. There are two types: free falling and parachuting.

Parachuting

After the free fall, it is time to open the parachute. This part of the jump is called parachuting.

The parachute is also called the canopy

Mental aspects

You need to be brave to jump out of an aircraft.

Skydiving builds confidence.

EARLY HISTORY

Parachuting began in the 15th century, when Italian artist and inventor, Leonardo da Vinci sketched a parachute in his notebook.

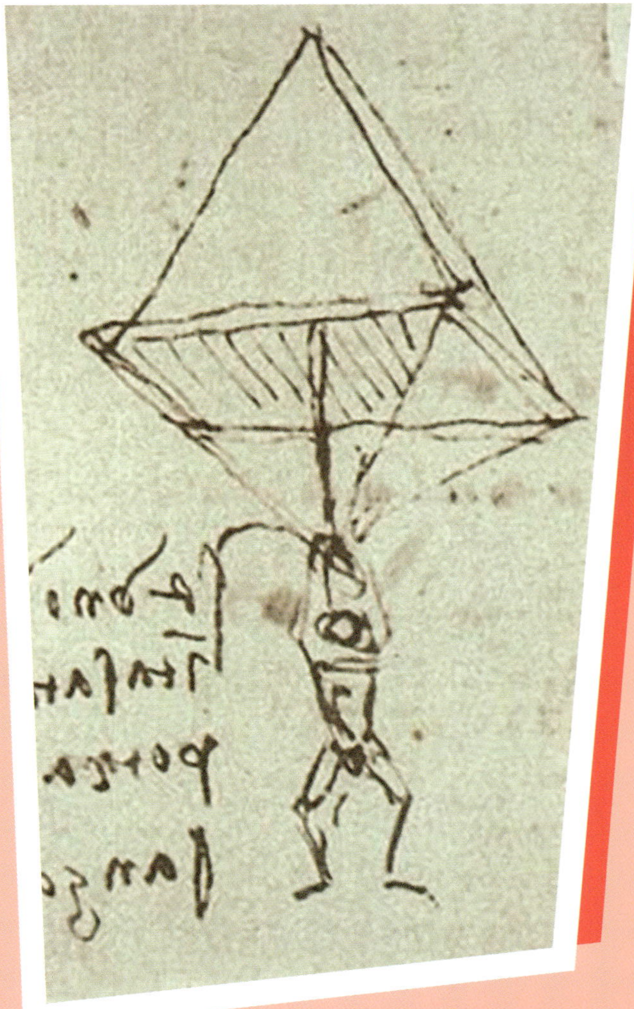

Leonardo da Vinci's parachute sketch (1483)

Leonardo's parachute was made of cloth over a pyramid-shaped frame. His idea was to help people to escape from burning buildings.

Sébastien Lenormand parachuted from the Montpelier Observatory in Paris, France in 1783.

Sébastien first used the word **parachute.** This French word means 'to shield a fall'.

Sébastien Lenormand parachuting from the Montpelier Observatory

Some early balloonists tried their parachutes out on dogs.

Others leapt from hot-air balloons.

An early parachute jump from a hot-air balloon

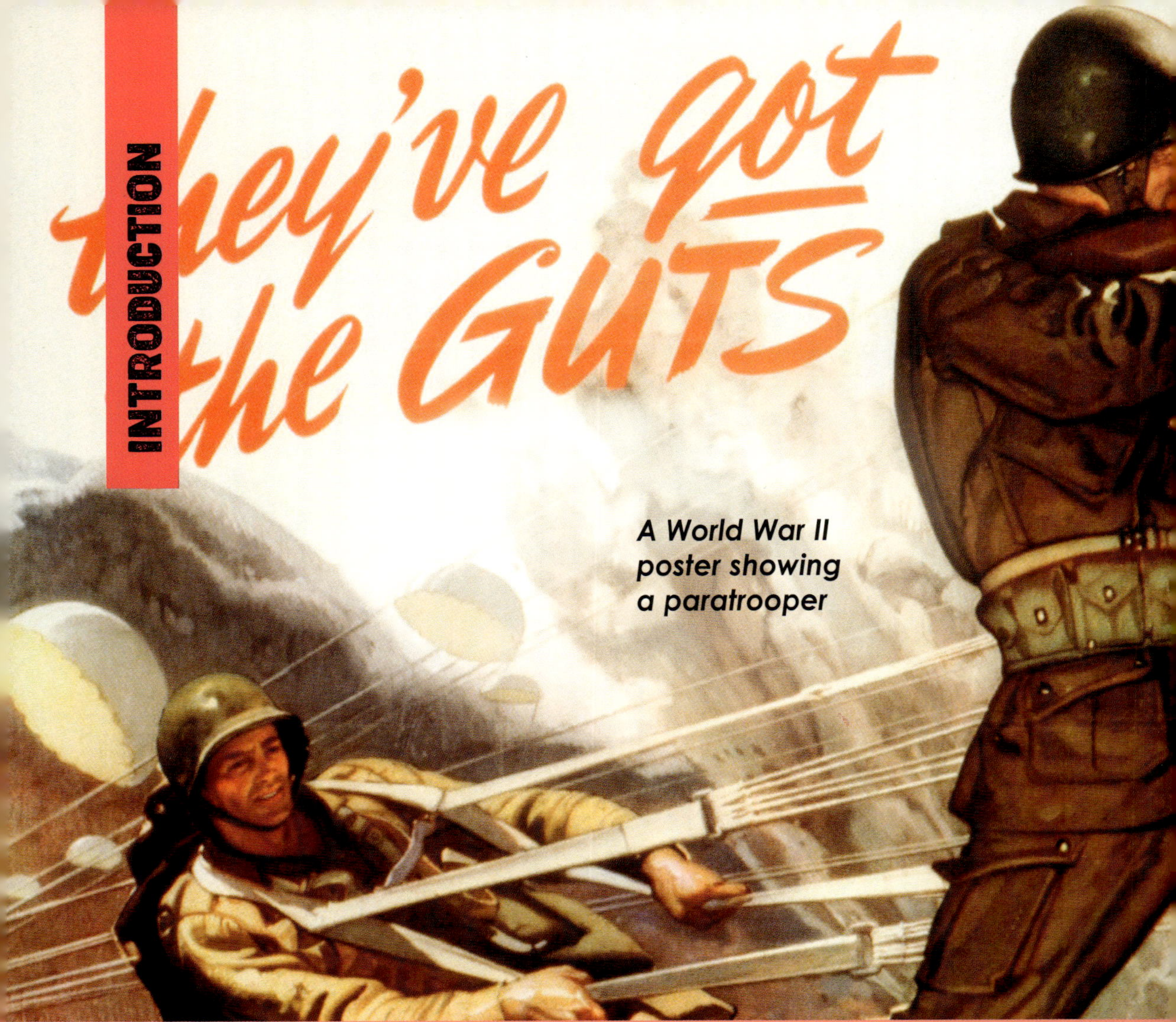

A World War II poster showing a paratrooper

THE FIRST FREE FALL

Until the 20th century, people thought you would black out in free fall. Georgia 'Tiny' Broadwick discovered this was untrue.

Tiny started parachuting in 1907 as a carnival act. She was only 14. Tiny went up attached to a balloon, released her parachute and floated down.

Georgia 'Tiny' Broadwick

Käthe Paulus designed a parachute for the German air force. In World War I, every German pilot was given one.

Léo Valentin in an early wingsuit

Militaries in other parts of the world began using parachutes.

The US Army added a second parachute in case the first failed.

DEVELOPMENTS

In the 1950s, silk parachutes were given holes to create forward speed. This led to sport parachutes with a strange pattern of holes (see above).

Ram-air

In the 1950s, Domina Jalbert invented the ram-air – a rectangular parachute.

In the 1970s, the ram-air became the main parachute. Round parachutes were used as the reserve parachute.

In the 1980s, the ram-air design was used for reserves.

Originally ram-air parachutes had five-cells

A modern nine-cell ram-air parachute

Sport

By the 1990s, parachutes had nine cells.

Many developments in parachuting took place in the 1990s. Parachuting is now a popular sport.

PARACHUTES

A modern ram-air parachute is inflated with air through the openings at the front of the cells. These cells are closed at the back, so the parachute is stable.

A ram-air parachute has a forward speed of about 25–30 miles per hour (40–50 km/h). The forward speed keeps the canopy inflated.

A ram-air canopy is made from nylon and is covered with a special liquid

Venezuelan pro, Francisco Neri

Skydivers still use a reserve parachute.

The main and the reserve parachutes are packed together in one neat container.

Parachutes being packed

ACCESSORIES

Skydivers wear jumpsuits over their clothes. This stops loose material flapping over emergency handles.

Helmet

Helmets protect the head in case of collisions in the sky or hard landings.

Goggles protect the eyes from wind.

Goggles

Some people wear open-faced helmets with goggles instead of closed helmets.

Gloves

Thin leather gloves keep the hands warm, protect from line burns and give good grip.

Weights

Lighter jumpers wear lead weights so they fall faster. This helps them to fly in free fall at the same speed as heavier people.

Knife

Skydivers often carry a knife to cut through lines, in case they get tangled.

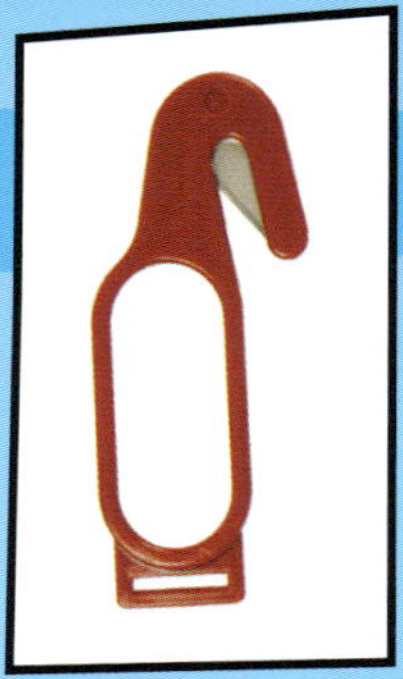

GADGETS

Cells

Each cell of the canopy is a different color.

Brake lines

These connect the back of the canopy to the toggles.

Harness

The pilot is strapped into the harness. It is connected to the main and reserve parachutes.

Toggles

These are the brakes of the parachute. Toggles can also be used to steer.

Most skydivers wear an automatic activation device (ADD). This operates the reserve if the main parachute fails.

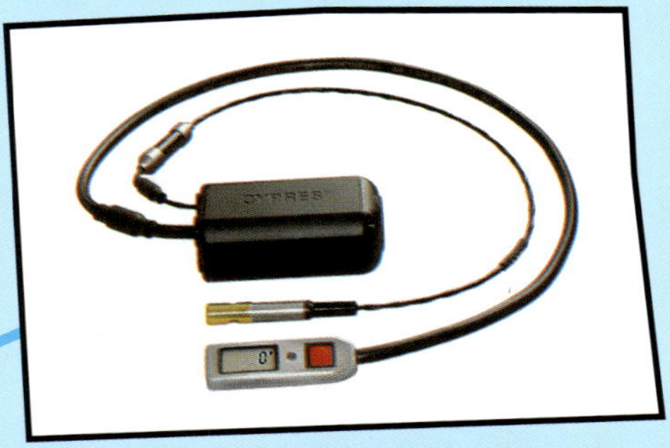

An automatic activation device

An altimeter

An altimeter shows the skydiver's height above the ground.

Recent technology includes a head-up display. The altitude and free-fall speed are projected into the view of the skydiver.

American, Craig Girard with a head-up altitude display

A paraski competition

ACCURACY

In accuracy competitions, each jumper tries to land as close to the target as possible. This is a tiny circle, about the size of a man's thumbnail.

If you land on the disc, you score a zero. If you land further away, the distance is your score.

At world level accuracy competitions there is often a jump-off between two competitors to decide the winner.

Vertical accuracy

Cheryl Stearns (USA)

In paraski competitions, entrants jump onto a ski slope and are scored for accuracy.

Then they slalom down a ski run and are scored on their times. The competitor with the highest combined score is the winner.

Cheryl Stearns is one of the most successful competitive skydivers of all time.

Her achievements include being a two-time Women's World Champion in style and accuracy parachuting, and smashing a total of 30 world records!

Extreme canopy piloting by Jay Moledzki (Canada)

CANOPY PILOTING

Canopy piloting competitions have three areas: speed, distance and zone accuracy. In speed, the canopy pilots are scored on how fast they go.

After the skydive, they open their canopies and fly in a series of spirals, to build up speed.

Freestyle canopy piloting by Ian Bobo (USA)

Freestyle is creative canopy piloting. The pilot can create new artistic moves in the air.

Jonathan Tagle (USA)

Jonathan Tagle started skydiving at age 31. He did 800 jumps in his first year. He completed over 8,000 jumps, before his death in 2012.

In 2005, he was overall world champion in canopy piloting.

CANOPY FORMATION

Single canopies can be linked together in many ways. You can join them on top of one another, side by side or you can combine the two methods and build amazing formations.

A rotation (formation) competition team

There are speed competitions where the aim is to join together the fastest.

81 canopies

The best way to build a large formation is in a diamond. A diamond is very stable.

The world record of a canopy formation of 100 people was set in 2007.

THE STABLE POSITION

If you go into free fall curled up in a ball, you will tumble. But if you make your body streamlined, you can fly without spinning or rolling over. This is called the stable position.

The usual skydiving position is belly-to-earth, as shown above. The body acts like a shuttlecock.

A shuttlecock falling downwards; the arrows show the air flow

Skydivers usually jump at 13,000 feet (3,962 m), free fall for one minute, then open their parachutes at 2,500 feet (762 m).

In a free fall dive, you can reach 200 miles per hour (320 km/h)!

Stable position

Once you can fall in the stable position, it is easy to change the angle of your body to move it through the air.

FORMATION SKYDIVING

Joining together in free fall is called formation skydiving.

Speed

The simplest competition is speed. The winning team is the fastest to build a formation.

The British eight-way team

Teams

Teams contain four or eight people. They leave the aircraft linked together.

Claire 'Sparky' Scott

Claire is the only woman to have won five world titles in four-way formation skydiving.

Sparky gained her nickname by flying into power lines and cutting off electricity to a whole village!

British skydiver, Claire 'Sparky' Scott

LARGE FORMATIONS

It is possible to build very large formations. As of 2021, the world record stands at 400 skydivers!

World record

In 2006, five enormous aircraft, taking 80 people each, were used for the world record. The jump was from 23,000 feet (7,010 m). The record included jumpers from 40 different countries.

Women's world record

The current record (2021) for an all-female formation was set in 2009 in California, USA, by 181 women from around the world.

Five Hercules planes load for the largest formation world record attempt in 2006

FREEFLYING

Flying in free fall in non-belly-to-earth positions is called freeflying.

Freefly competitions involve teams of three. One person wears a camera, and the other two skydivers perform together.

A totem: one freeflyer stands on another's shoulders

Judges score the routine on its technical and artistic content.

The head-down position is popular when freeflying because it is fast.

There is less time in free fall before you need to turn belly-to-earth and open the parachute.

The head-down position

TANDEM SKYDIVING

The three ways to start skydiving are tandem, AFF and static line.

A tandem jump is in a dual harness with an instructor.

A tandem parachute and harness is made for two. A complete beginner jumps with an instructor.

Tandems leave the aircraft at around 12,000 feet (3,657 m) and free fall for 30 seconds.

A tandem instructor (top) and beginner (bottom)

In a tandem jump, the instructor opens the canopy at about 5,000 feet (1,524 m).

A tandem landing

ACCELERATED FREE FALL (AFF)

An AFF jump is with an instructor on either side in free fall.

The instructors communicate to the beginner with hand signals

AFF jumps

The first AFF jump is from 12,000 feet (3,657 m) with two instructors, one on either side.

The beginner opens the parachute at 5,000 feet (1,524 m).

Training

An AFF course takes one day of training. The full course is eight to ten jumps. The first three jumps are with two instructors. After that, there is only one instructor.

Qualifying

Every AFF course is adapted to suit the individual skydiver. Sometimes the jumps are filmed.

STATIC LINE AND TUNNELS

A static line jump is on your own. Adults can do a static line jump from around 3,500 feet (1,066 m).

The static line is attached to the aircraft. It automatically opens the parachute.

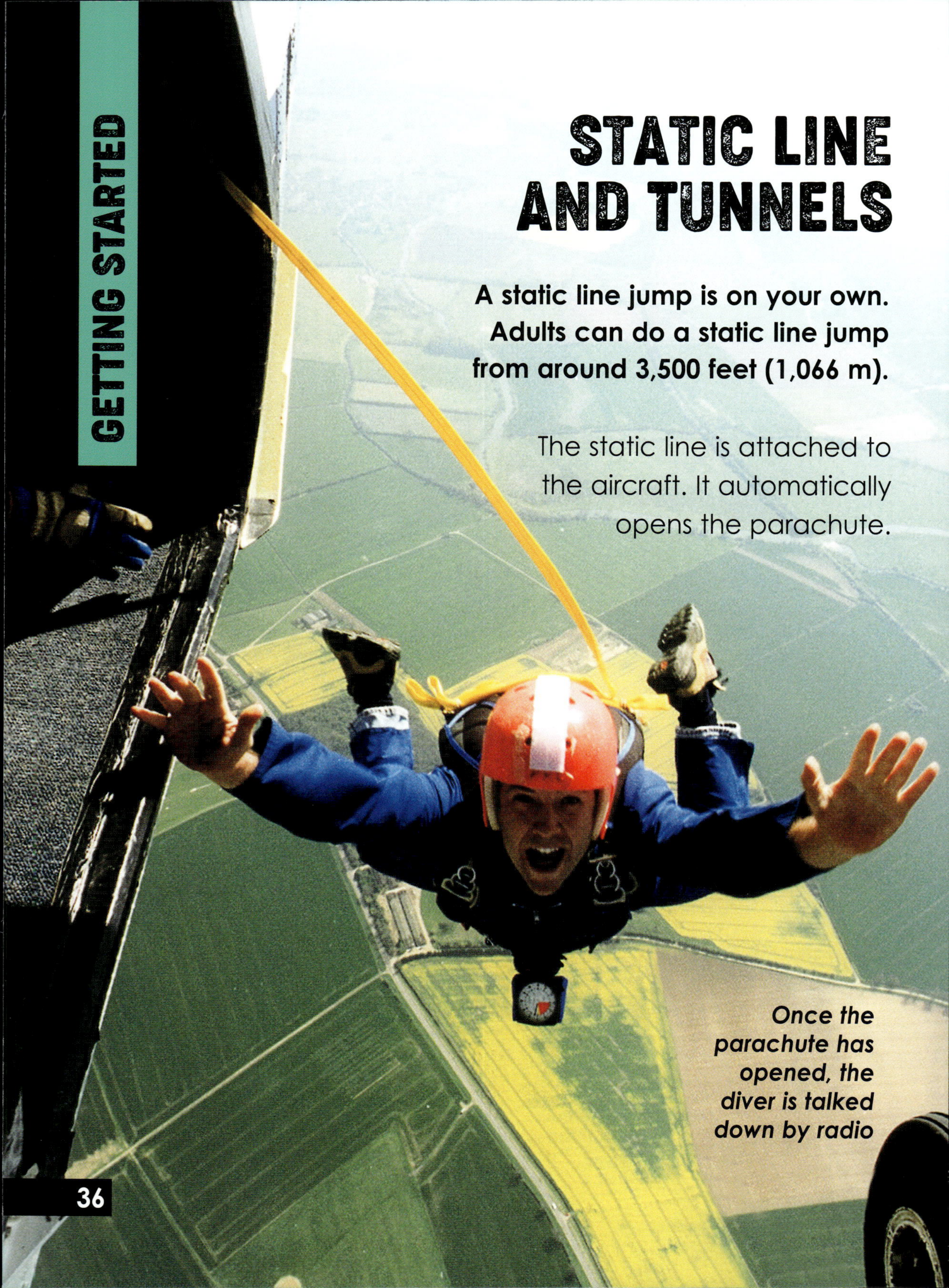

Once the parachute has opened, the diver is talked down by radio

The first free fall is five seconds

First free fall

People who want to take up skydiving do another five to ten static-line jumps.

If these are good, they are cleared for their first AFF jump.

Wind tunnels

Vertical wind tunnels simulate free fall. Skydivers use them to practice competition routines.

They are fantastic if you want to learn to skydive.

A tunnel-flying skydiver

World champion in 1999 and 2001, sky surfer Tanya Garcia-O'Brien (USA)

SKY SURFING

Sky surfers ride waves on surfboards thousands of feet up in the air.

Sky surfing competition teams consist of a sky surfer and a camera flier.

Judges score the routine on creativity, originality and difficulty. Judges also score the filming.

A sky surfer with a boogie board

Sky surfboards look like skateboards, but there are removable attachments for the feet.

BASE JUMPING

BASE jumping is skydiving from a fixed object.

BASE jumping is more dangerous than normal skydiving. Jumpers do not use a reserve parachute and they can collide with the object they are jumping from.

Austrian, Felix Baumgartner prepares to jump from the Christ the Redeemer statue in Rio de Janeiro, Brazil

Jumping off the Eiger Mushroom in Switzerland

Climb to jump

Climbing the object is part of the adventure and gives a good workout before the jump.

The Pit of the Swallows has 80,000 birds living in it

Underground skydiving

A cave in Mexico allows skydivers to jump underground!

You have to fly in a constant spiral to avoid hitting the walls.

WINGSUITS

We now have wingsuits that double the free fall time.

The modern birdman has one huge wing stretching from the wrists to the ankles. The large wing creates forward movement like a sail. The result is a long flight at a slow speed.

Flocks

Birdmen fly in formations called flocks. The wingsuits double the free fall time to enjoy whizzing around the sky.

Ways to fly

Wingsuits are used by both skydivers and BASE jumpers and contain parachutes for a safe landing.

STUNTS

In 1998, Bruno Brokken and Richie Hornig flew their canopies under Besalu Bridge in Spain for the film, Crosswind.

It took precise timing and control for the skydivers to avoid hitting the sides of the bridge.

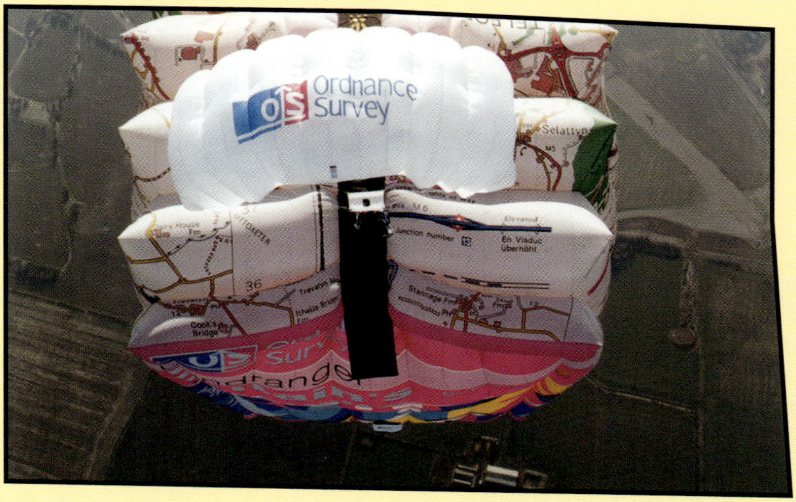

Dave Morris landing on the hot-air balloon

Balloon landing

In 2001, Dave Morris skydived from a helicopter at 10,000 feet (3,048 m) and opened his canopy. He landed on top of a hot-air balloon at 5,000 feet (1,524 m). Dave then jumped off the top of the balloon. He went into free fall for the second time in one skydive!

Adrian Nicholas and the da Vinci parachute

Da Vinci parachute

In 2000, Adrian Nicholas launched Leonardo da Vinci's 500 year-old parachute idea.

The da Vinci parachute was launched from a hot-air balloon at 10,000 feet (3,048 m) over South Africa.

GLOSSARY

Birdman Someone who skydives in a wingsuit. An old fashioned term for anyone who made wings and tried to fly.

Boogie board A short, light surfboard, ridden lying face down.

Cells Each section of a ram-air canopy.

Cutaway Getting rid of the main canopy, usually when it has not opened properly, or is tangled around something or someone.

Emergency handles These are located on the parachute harness for use if things go wrong.

Extreme canopy piloting Flying a parachute to gain maximum performance, usually making a complete spiral or two with the canopy to build up speed.

Formation Two or more jumpers linked in free fall (formation skydiving) or under a canopy (canopy formation).

Freefly To free fall any way other than belly-to-earth.

Lines Pieces of thin cord that attach the parachute to the harness, similar to guy lines on a tent.

Paratrooper A soldier trained in parachuting. Paratroopers were first used extensively in World War II by Germany.

Pilot The person controlling the parachute (or aircraft).

Ram-air An aerofoil parachute, open at the front and closed at the back. It is rammed full of air and becomes a solid flying wing. Its shape is rectangular but slightly curved.

Reserve A second parachute worn in case the first (main) parachute does not open properly.

Rotation One rotation is when the top person in a stack collapses his or her canopy, falls past everyone else and joins the stack at the bottom.

Slalom A ski race down a winding course marked by flags or poles.

Stack A formation where ram-air canopies are linked vertically above one another. The top jumper's feet are hooked into the bottom person's lines.

Static line A line attached to the aircraft that pulls the main parachute out and open as the jumper leaves the plane.

Wingsuit A jumpsuit with fabric between the legs and arms. It increases lift and free-fall time.

INDEX